◆ Personal, Moral, S[ocial] and Cultural education

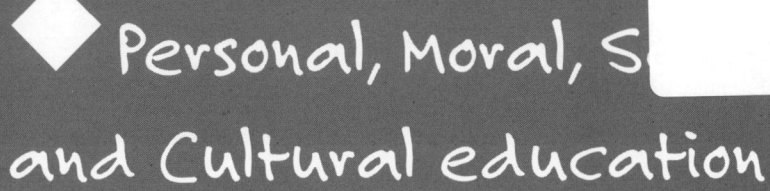

GROWING UP TODAY
Caring for the environment

Key Stage 1/P1-3

Ros Bayley and Lynn Broadbent

HOPSCOTCH EDUCATIONAL PUBLISHING

Acknowledgements

Published by Hopscotch Educational Publishing Company Ltd, Althorpe House, Althorpe Street, Leamington Spa CV31 2AU.

© 1999 Hopscotch Educational Publishing

Written by Ros Bayley and Lynn Broadbent
Cover design by Kim Ashby
Page design by Steve Williams
Illustrated by Cathy Gilligan
Cover illustration by Cathy Gilligan
Printed by Clintplan, Southam

Ros Bayley and Lynn Broadbent hereby assert their moral right to be identified as the authors of this work in accordance with the Copyright, Designs and Patents Act, 1988.

ISBN 1-902239-37-7

All rights reserved. This book is sold subject to the condition that it shall not, by way of trade or otherwise, be lent, hired out or otherwise circulated without the publisher's prior consent in any form or binding or cover other than that in which it is published and without a similar condition, including this condition, being imposed upon the subsequent purchaser.

No part of this publication may be reproduced, stored in a retrieval system, or transmitted, in any form or by any means, electronic, mechanical photocopying, recording or otherwise, without the prior permission of the publisher, except where photocopying for educational purposes within the school or other educational establishment that has purchased this book is expressly permitted in the text.

Contents

Introduction	4
Respect for living things	6
The importance of things of beauty	11
Working together	16
Caring for our planet	21
People and the environment	26
Respect for habitats	31
Preserving the environment for future generations	36
Responsibility for other species	41
Generic sheets	
Acting responsibly	46
Damage to the environment	47

Introduction

Our overriding intention in writing this book is to enable the children to explore the importance of the environment as the basis of life and a source of wonder and inspiration. When children acquire this basic understanding, it becomes much easier for them to value the natural world and appreciate that we all have responsibility to maintain a sustainable environment for future generations.

We live in a time when the world is changing at an alarming rate. If environmental destruction continues at its present rate it is estimated that by the year 2020 the only wilderness remaining will be in national parks and reserves. At the current pace of change it is also possible that a quarter of our present plant and animal species will be extinct. As Jennie Baker points out in her notes to 'Window', "Already, at least two species become extinct each hour." By sharing such books with the children we can help them to understand that we have a responsibility to other species and for ensuring that development can be justified.

In our choice of books we have attempted to strike a balance between those that focus on global issues and those that have their roots closer to home. Through this dual approach we aim to help the children understand their place within nature and to foster their awareness of being part of the web of life.

In 'Danny's Duck', 'Billy's Sunflower' and 'The Smallest Whale', the children are able to see the way in which it is possible for a young child to make a positive contribution to the environment, and this is really important. If we are to care genuinely about the world in which we live it is first necessary that we understand the way in which we personally affect the environment. It is only when we understand this that we can change the way we do things and subsequently make a difference. The remaining focus books ask the children to explore environmental issues in a broader context.

Never has there been a more urgent need to heighten children's awareness of man's responsibility for the Earth. We are faced with enormous issues for which there is no quick fix. The life system of our planet is under increasing threat and how we now choose to treat the Earth will have far-reaching consequences for the future. The children are faced with the question of whether our planet will be able to continue to support human life.

It falls to us as teachers to help the children to understand these important environmental issues and support them in exploring what they want for the future. Only then will they be able to see how they might make a personal contribution to this process.

BIBLIOGRAPHY OF TITLES REFERRED TO IN THIS BOOK

'Danny's Duck' by June Crebbin (Walker Books)

'Billy's Sunflower' by Nicola Moon (Scholastic, Little Hippo)

'The Smallest Whale' by Elizabeth Beresford (Orchard Picture Books)

'Dinosaurs and All That Rubbish' by Michael Foreman (Picture Puffin)

'Window' by Jenny Baker (Red Fox)

'The Great Green Forest' by Paul Geraghty (Red Fox)

'Where the Forest Meets the Sea' by Jeannie Baker (Walker Books)

'The Hunter' by Paul Geraghty (Red Fox)

◆Respect for living things

FOCUS BOOK

DANNY'S DUCK
by June Crebbin
Walker Books

INTENDED LEARNING

◆ To help the children consider the importance of caring for and appreciating living things.
◆ To provide an opportunity for them to reflect upon their personal responsibilities with regard to this process.

Synopsis of the story

One day as Danny stares out of the classroom window looking for aeroplanes he notices a duck fly into the playground. No one sees her come except Danny. When playtime arrives Danny sets off in search of the duck and finds her nesting in a pile of leaves and twigs. Upon returning to school he paints a picture of the duck on her nest. Next time he visits the nest he finds nine eggs and again he paints a picture to show what he has seen. Each day he visits the nest until one day he arrives to find it empty. At first he is really upset, but his distress turns to delight when his teacher, who realises what has happened, takes him to a nearby pond where they find the duck with her nine baby ducklings.

Notes for teachers

'Danny's Duck' is an excellent book for helping children to be aware of the importance of respecting and caring for living things. It can heighten their awareness of the need to leave natural things alone and help them to understand the process of change and the transient nature of the natural world. Danny takes great delight in this process and respectfully appreciates being the only person to know about the duck.

This beautiful book shows, through both the text and its illustrations, the way in which the natural world touches our emotions and shows how, as human beings, we sometimes need to represent and describe this process.

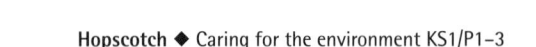

Methodology

Having shared this book with the children, set the scene for discussion by drawing their attention to the illustrations and asking the following questions.

Questions to ask

- What can you see in these pictures that tell us that the adults and children at this school care about the environment and the natural world?
- Show them the picture of Danny looking out of the window and ask them why they think Danny was so interested in looking out of the window? What was he looking for?
- Danny searches for the duck at playtime. Can you think of some words that would describe his feelings when he finds her?
- Although the duck sees Danny, she doesn't fly away. Why do you think this is?
- When Danny goes back into school he draws the duck but he doesn't tell anybody about what he has seen. Why do you think this is?
- Although Danny visited the duck every day nobody else knew she was there. Why do you think this was?
- When Danny found the empty nest he burst into tears. Why did he do this? What did he think had happened?
- Draw the children's attention to Danny's painting and ask: What does Danny's painting show?
- Show the picture of Danny and his teacher by the empty nest. Ask: Do you think Danny knows what has happened to the duck and her eggs?
- When Danny sees the duck he shouts, 'There's my duck.' Why does he say this?
- What do you think will happen next?

Encourage the children to relate the story to their own experience. Ask:
- What would you have done if you had found the nest?
- Has anything like this ever happened to you?
- How might the story have been different if Danny had behaved differently, for example if he had interfered with the nest or touched the duck?
- Have you helped living things, such as feeding birds or helping an animal?

The photocopiable activity sheets

Which can you touch? This activity requires the children to think carefully about what they should or should not touch. It requires no formal reading or writing skills.

What could you do? In this activity the children are asked to write a sentence explaining why they would take a certain course of action. This could be undertaken as a group exercise and be scribed by an adult.

What would you say? This sheet is more demanding and requires the children to be able to think and write independently.

◆ Which can you touch? ◆

◆ Cut out these pictures and sort them into two groups:
Group 1 – Things you can touch.
Group 2 – Things you should leave alone.

What could you do?

◆ Look at these pictures. Draw a picture in the empty box to show what you could do to help.

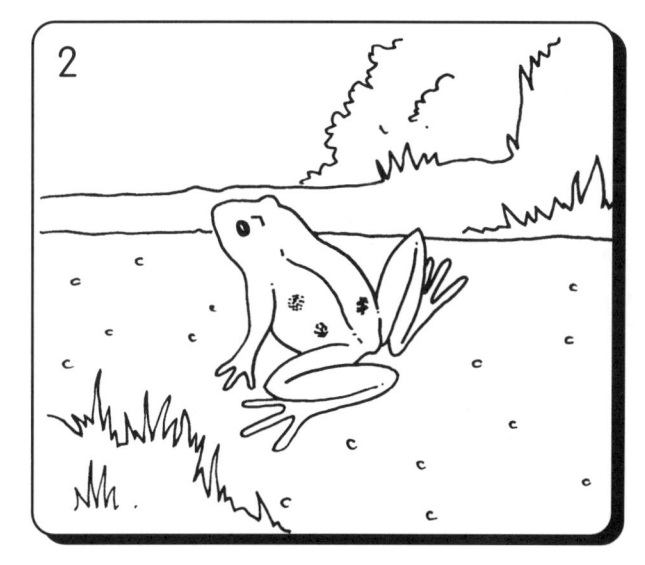

◆ Write a sentence to explain why you would do this.

_____

_____

_____

Hopscotch ◆ Caring for the environment KS1/P1–3   PHOTOCOPIABLE PAGE   9

◆ What would you say? ◆

◆ Look carefully at the picture.

◆ Write down what you might say to these children to stop them taking the ducklings out of the water.

_____
_____
_____
_____
_____
_____

◆ The importance of things of beauty

FOCUS BOOK

BILLY'S SUNFLOWER
by Nicola Moon
Scholastic, Little Hippo

INTENDED LEARNING

◆ To explore the ways in which living things are subject to constant change and how this can sometimes present us with difficulties, especially where we have invested time and care in them.

Synopsis of the story

Billy had grown a beautiful sunflower from seed. He had watched it grow taller and taller until it became as tall as the sky. Each day he admired its beauty until one day he noticed that its leaves didn't seem quite so golden. Billy's sunflower was dying.

Billy tried to save it by watering it, but to no avail. By the next day it was wrinkly and droopy. The rest of the story deals with Billy's feelings as he begins to understand the inevitable cycle of life and death. The story ends on a high when, in spite of his intense sadness, Billy realises that his flower is 'raining seeds'. He collects the seeds to feed to the birds but carefully selects the five largest ones to plant the following Spring.

Notes for teachers

This is an excellent book for helping children to explore the ways in which our interactions with the environment can evoke strong feelings. It focuses on the importance of things of beauty in our lives and addresses issues around life cycles in nature. It is sensitively written and illustrated and explores emotions with which most young children will be able to identify. It clarifies the process of constant change within the natural world and can really help the children in coming to terms with the transient nature of some of the things they find beautiful.

Methodology

By sharing 'Billy's Sunflower' with the children we can provide them with an opportunity to reflect upon the awe and wonder that we can experience as we interact with the natural world. A useful starting point is to explore how Billy felt about his sunflower as he watched it grow.

Questions to ask

- Why did Billy think his sunflower was beautiful? Ask the children to identify the words in the text that describe his feelings.
- When Billy watched his sunflower growing do you think he understood that one day it would die?
- What did he think was happening when his sunflower began to look different?
- How did he feel about what was happening to his sunflower? Try to extend the children's vocabulary beyond 'sad'. Introduce words like 'anxious', 'confused' and 'bewildered'.
- Billy's sister told him about autumn and said that his flower would die. Do you think Billy would understand what autumn was?
- The author says 'a gust of wind rustled in the dying leaves as if the flower was trying to speak'. If the flower had been able to speak what do you think it might have said to Billy?
- Show the children the picture of Billy's face as the seeds fell. Ask them if they can think of some words to describe the way Billy is feeling. (Here, again, try to extend their vocabulary beyond 'happy'.)
- As he gathered up the seeds why did Billy pick out the biggest seeds to save?
- How did Billy feel as he watched the birds feeding on the sunflower seeds? (This is a good time to help the children reflect upon the way in which the death of one thing can nourish the life of another species.)
- How did Billy feel at the end of the book?
- Encourage the children to relate the story to their own experience. They should be able to talk about things in the natural world that they have appreciated and enjoyed and about their feelings when things have changed.

The photocopiable activity sheets

Growing and changing This sheet requires no reading but may need to be supported by some initial discussion. It is intended to help the children focus on the life cycle of the sunflower.

Looking at beautiful things In this activity the children are asked to express opinions and preferences. Following some initial explanation it can be undertaken independently.

Beautiful things This sheet is slightly more demanding. It requires the children to think reflectively and write independently.

Growing and changing

◆ Cut out the pictures and put them in order to show how a sunflower changes as it grows.

Hopscotch ◆ Caring for the environment KS1/P1–3   PHOTOCOPIABLE PAGE

Looking at beautiful things

◆ Cut out the pictures and put them in order to show which you like the most. Underneath each picture write a word to describe how each scene would make you feel. Compare your finished work with your friends.

PHOTOCOPIABLE PAGE

Hopscotch ◆ Caring for the environment KS1/P1–3

Beautiful things

◆ Draw pictures of things from the natural world that affect the way you feel.

◆ Write a sentence to describe the way these things make you feel.

_____

_____

_____

Hopscotch ◆ Caring for the environment KS1/P1–3   PHOTOCOPIABLE   PAGE   15

Working together

FOCUS BOOK

THE SMALLEST WHALE
by Elizabeth Beresford
Orchard Picture Books

INTENDED LEARNING

◆ To enhance the children's understanding of the way in which collaboration between individuals is sometimes necessary when addressing environmental issues.

Synopsis of the story

'The Smallest Whale' is a save-the-whale story based on a real event which happened off the island of Alderney in the Channel Islands. A school of whales were swimming up the English Channel when one of them was diverted off course by the sound of a fishing boat. The young whale followed the fishing boat and unfortunately was heading straight for the harbour. Unable to stop himself he was washed up onto the beach where he lay paralysed. The rest of the story revolves around the way that Josh, who had been on the fishing boat with his father, engages the whole community in working together to keep the whale wet and alive until high tide when it could be refloated.

Notes for teachers

This story contrasts well with 'Danny's Duck' (Chapter 1, page 6) as it calls for a completely different response from the main character. Whereas Danny needed to take a non-interventional approach and keep people away from his duck, Josh has to intervene and mobilise his entire community into helping him save the whale.

The story affords us further opportunities for exploring the theme of respect for living things and also provides an example of how a community can work together to address an environmental need. The emphasis is on action rather than being passive, and on the group rather than the individual.

Methodology

Although the story gives some incidental information about whales, it may be helpful to have some non-fiction material available to enable the children to access further information and support them with their learning. Clarify the children's understanding of what happened by asking the following questions.

Questions to ask

- Why did the whale follow the fishing boat?
- Why would the young whale die if he was left on the beach?
- Some children may not understand the way tides work and may need to be supported. Ask: What did Josh's father mean when he said, 'He'll dry and die if we leave him till the next high tide'?
- Josh really wanted to help the whale. Can you think of some words that would describe the way he was feeling when the whale was washed up on the beach?
- What did Josh do to get help for the whale? What places did he go to?
- For how long did the people need to keep the whale wet? Was it a long time?
- Josh got lots of people to help him. Could he have kept the whale wet by himself?
- Josh's dad said, 'I don't know if he is going to last until the tide comes in again.' Why did he say this?
- What were the rest of the whale family doing while all of this was going on?
- When the tide came back in, Josh's dad said that the whale would need some help. Ask: When the tide came in why could the whale not get back into the water by himself?
- Everybody helped. Could Josh and his father have got the whale back into the water on their own?
- How did the people feel as the smallest whale swam back to his family?

Encourage the children to identify all the different people who were involved in rescuing the whale.

The photocopiable activity sheets

Who could help? This activity is designed to challenge children's thinking and there are no right or wrong answers. It does not involve any writing.

How could you help? For this activity the children will need to look at the illustration very closely and engage in some hypothetical problem solving! They will need to be able to write independently or someone will need to scribe for them.

What can they do? To complete this activity the children will need to be able to write independently. It is designed to get them thinking about how each individual can make a contribution to improving the environment.

Who could help?

◆ Draw pictures to show who you could find to help you to rescue these animals.

18   PHOTOCOPIABLE PAGE   Hopscotch ◆ Caring for the environment KS1/P1–3

◆ How could you help? ◆

◆ Make a list of the jobs that need to be done to make this garden into a place that people can use and enjoy. List the people who could help get the job done.

JOBS TO BE DONE

_____

_____

_____

_____

_____

_____

_____

PEOPLE WHO COULD HELP

_____

_____

_____

_____

_____

_____

_____

Hopscotch ◆ Caring for the environment KS1/P1–3   PHOTOCOPIABLE PAGE

◆ What can they do? ◆

◆ This park is in urgent need of attention. Think about what the people in the picture could do to help make this park into a place where people would like to go. Write your answers below.

The children could _____

_____

The teenagers could _____

_____

The man could _____

_____

The lady could _____

_____

PHOTOCOPIABLE PAGE   Hopscotch ◆ Caring for the environment KS1/P1–3

◆Caring for our planet

FOCUS BOOK

DINOSAURS AND ALL THAT RUBBISH
by Michael Foreman
Picture Puffin

INTENDED LEARNING

◆ To raise the children's awareness of the ways in which the needs of man should be balanced against the needs of the environment. To enhance their understanding of how preserving and sustaining our environment has implications for all of us.

Synopsis of the story

One day, Man saw a beautiful star and all he could think about was getting to that star. In order to do this he built factories where a rocket could be built, but by the time it was finished everywhere was piled high with heaps of waste. The smouldering waste woke up the dinosaurs who, appalled by the state of the planet, set to work to clean up all the mess. When Man landed on his star he was disappointed to find there was nothing there so he set off for another star, only to find he had returned to earth. The dinosaurs decided to let him stay when he agreed that the Earth should be shared and enjoyed by everyone.

Notes for teachers

This is a modern fable with several issues running through the story. It asks us to reflect upon our collective responsibility for the planet on which we live and requires that we consider the balance between our own needs and those of the environment. It also raises issues around the disposal of waste and the exercise of power and control.

'Dinosaurs and All That Rubbish' is an age-appropriate vehicle for exploring the way in which power and greed can sometimes blind us to the wider needs of the environment in which we live.

Methodology

To get the most out of this book it is best used in conjunction with an environmental project, such as a school litter campaign or work on the local area. This enables the children to link the issues in the story with a meaningful 'real life' situation.

Before launching in with questions of our own we need to check out the children's understanding of the story. It is a good idea to ask an open-ended question like:

◆ Why do you think the author wanted to write this story?
◆ Why was the man so interested in the star?

The man realised that the only way to get there would be in a rocket. Ask the children the following questions.

Questions to ask

◆ What did he have to do in order to build a rocket?
◆ Did the man notice what was happening to the Earth as he built his rocket? (The illustrations may help the children with this question.)
◆ The man thought he would be happy when he reached the star. How did he feel when he got there?
◆ He then decided to go to another star. What do you think he hoped to find there?
◆ How did the dinosaurs feel when they saw what had happened to the Earth? (With some classes it may be worth asking them to think about how the dinosaurs would feel if they came back to our world as it is today.)
◆ The author tells us that as the rubbish was cleared 'a fresh new forest of flowers and trees spread like a smile around the world'. Why did the author use those words to describe what was happening?
◆ When the man's rocket lands, where does he think he is?
◆ When the man tells the dinosaur that the 'paradise' belongs to him, how does the dinosaur reply?
◆ The man says that you need a big brain to look after the planet, but the dinosaur says you need a big heart. What does he mean by this?
◆ The dinosaur told the man that the Earth belongs to all of us and that we should all look after it and care for it. In what ways can you help to care for it?

The photocopiable activity sheets

Caring for our planet The children are asked to draw two pictures in response to this activity. They will need supporting with some initial discussion.

Things that help our planet This activity requires the children to think reflectively but involves no writing.

Showing that we care This is a more complex activity requiring independence in both thinking and writing.

Caring for our planet

◆ These children are caring for their environment.

◆ Draw some pictures to show some of the things you could do to help care for our planet.

Hopscotch ◆ Caring for the environment KS1/P1–3   PHOTOCOPIABLE PAGE

Things that help our planet

◆ Cut out the pictures and sort them into two groups.
Group 1 – Things that help the planet.
Group 2 – Things that damage the planet.

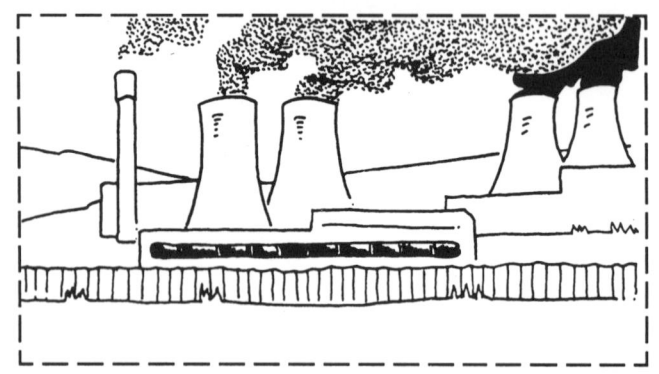

PHOTOCOPIABLE PAGE   Hopscotch ◆ Caring for the environment KS1/P1–3

◆ Showing that we care ◆

◆ Look carefully at the picture. Put a circle around the parts of the picture you would like to change.

◆ Write some sentences to describe what you would do to change this park into one that is cared for.

_____

_____

_____

_____

_____

_____

Hopscotch ◆ Caring for the environment KS1/P1–3   PHOTOCOPIABLE   PAGE   25

People and the environment

FOCUS BOOK
WINDOW
by Jenny Baker
Red Fox

INTENDED LEARNING

◆ To enhance the children's understanding of the ways in which development impacts on the environment.
◆ To be able to identify some of the things that are 'lost' in this process.
◆ To encourage the children to begin to think about ways in which environmental destruction might be avoided.

Synopsis of the story

'Window' is a picture book without text. It tells the story of how a landscape changes over a period of 24 years. The book consists of a series of collages seen by looking out through a window. In the first picture a mother is holding her baby as she looks out over unspoiled countryside. The subsequent pictures show how the view changes as the baby grows into a man. The story ends as it began but this time it is the man who stands in the window. He is now holding his own baby as he looks out over a site that is about to be developed.

Notes for teachers

This picture book depicts the process of environmental destruction without using any text. The collages are packed with detail and really encourage the children to think about the way in which the intervention of the human race can dramatically change the environment in a very short space of time. It helps the children to understand how we are changing our world at an alarming rate.

By sharing 'Window' with the children we can encourage them to think about how people's needs impact on the environment and begin to question whether development can always be justified.

Methodology

This book shows 24 years of someone's life in as many pages, although this may not be immediately apparent to some of the children. It is a complex book. At the same time as depicting the process of environmental destruction, it chronicles somebody's life from birth to adulthood.

Questions to ask

- Show the children the first illustration and ask them: What do you think this picture is about? Who is in the room? What can you see through the window?
- Show them the second page and ask: How have things changed inside the room? How have things changed outside the room?
- These questions will relate to almost every picture. As you go through the book and allow the children to absorb it, encourage them to identify and reflect upon the changes that are taking place. When they have looked at all the pictures ask: What is this book about?
- Encourage them to look at the pictures again. Ask: What wildlife can you see in each picture? What is happening to the wildlife as the boy grows up? Encourage them to notice the way in which the wild animals are replaced by domestic pets.
- Although it is not an environmental issue it is worth asking: What do we know about the boy in this story from looking at the pictures? What do you think he is interested in?
- Help the children to clarify what the last picture in the book is telling us. Ask: What do you think the man is thinking in the last picture in this book?
- As the boy in this story grows up into a man, many things change. Ask: Why does this happen? What do you think will happen to the world if things go on changing in this way? Do you think there is anything that can be done about this?
- Encourage the children to relate the book to their own experience. Ask: Has the landscape near your house changed? It may be possible to look at old photographs of the school.
- Do you think that the changes that have happened in the book are good changes?

The photocopiable activity sheets

Spot the difference This activity is intended to enhance children's awareness of how development changes landscape. It requires no reading or writing but is ideal for discussion in pairs or small groups.

What will happen next? In this activity the children are asked to speculate about how development might change a landscape. They are asked to write a simple sentence on their own.

The building site This activity has the same aim as the first two but is intended for children who can write independently and calls for a more complex response.

◆ Spot the difference! ◆

◆ Look at the two pictures. Use crayons or felt-tipped pens to show the things that have changed.

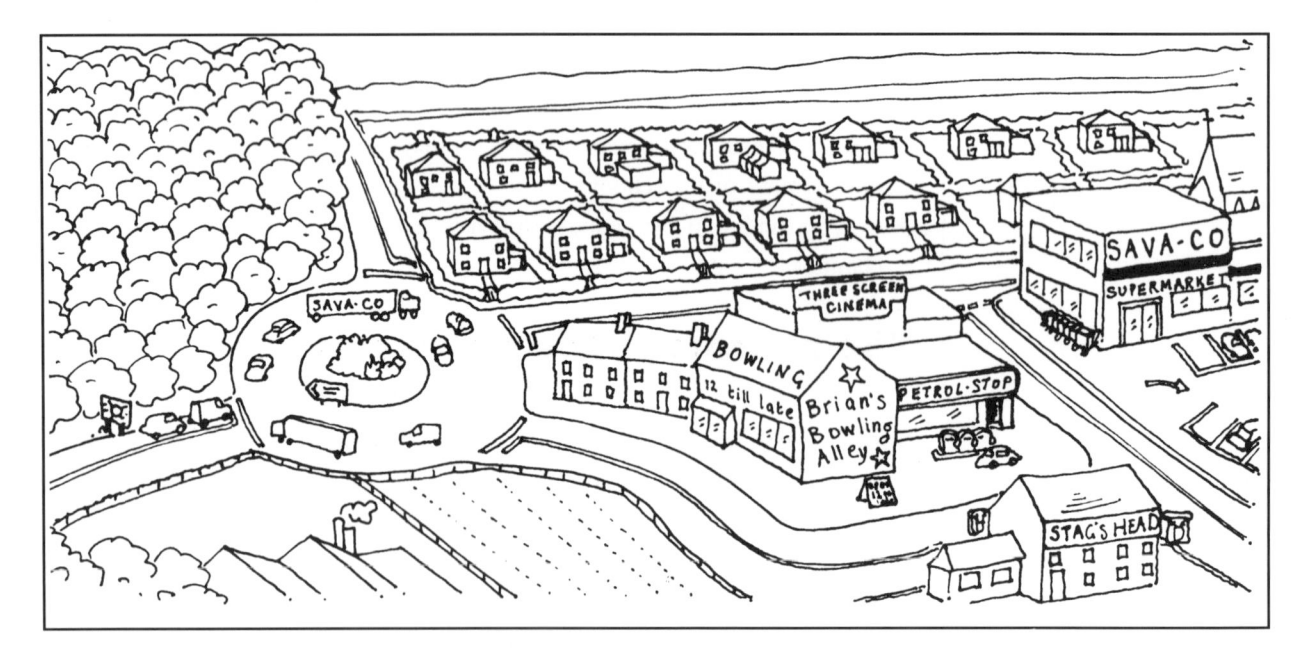

◆ Talk to your friend about what has happened and what you think may happen in the future.

28 PHOTOCOPIABLE PAGE Hopscotch ◆ Caring for the environment KS1/P1–3

What will happen next?

◆ Look at these two pictures. What has changed?

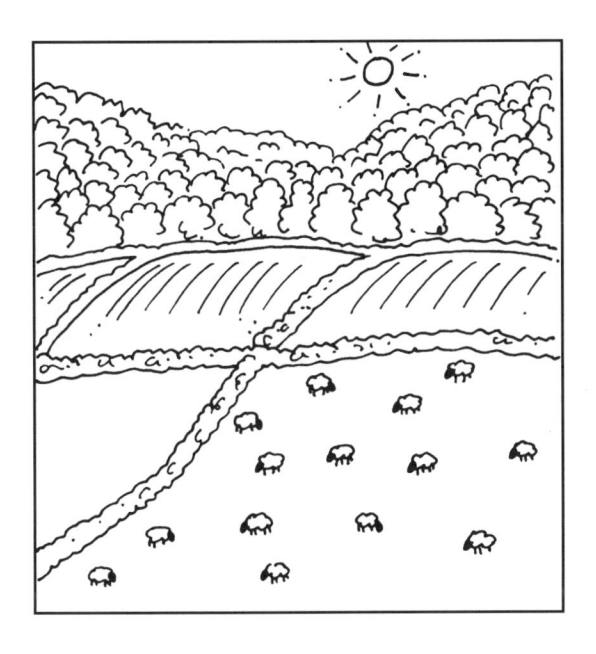

◆ Draw a picture to show what other things might change.

◆ Write a sentence to say why you think this will happen.

◆ The building site ◆

◆ A new housing estate is about to be built on this land. Think about how this will change the environment and all the things that will be lost.

◆ Pretend that you live across the road from this building site. Write a letter to your friend to tell them about what is happening and how you feel about this. Start your letter here and continue on the back of this sheet.

Dear _____
_____
_____
_____
_____
_____
_____

◆Respect for habitats

FOCUS BOOK

THE GREAT GREEN FOREST
by Paul Geraghty
Red Fox

INTENDED LEARNING

◆ To introduce the children to the idea that human development has consequences and that it impacts on the environment and the natural world.

◆ To encourage the children to think about our responsibilities in relation to other species and their habitats.

Synopsis of the story

The treemouse wants a nice quiet sleep in the great green forest. Unfortunately, her fellow creatures are making so much noise that she finds it impossible to rest. She repeatedly calls for silence, but none of the noises made by the animals is as disturbing as the silence that pervades the forest when a bulldozer begins to attack the trees. Unnerved by the silence and unaware of what is happening, the treemouse pleads for someone to make a noise. She waits, until with a great noise trees begin to fall to the ground. Sensing that 'her' tree will be next she yells out at the top of her voice. Suddenly, the driver of the bulldozer is aware of being observed by angry eyes and after reflecting on the devastation he has caused, goes away to leave the forest in peace.

Notes for teachers

This is an excellent story for helping children to reflect upon the implications of development on animal habitats. It encourages the children to question whether humans have the right to destroy animal habitats and cut down forests that may never be replaced. Through exploring this text children can begin to question human values in the context of the environment. 'The Great Green Forest' encourages us to look at whether the environment is of value for itself, or only for the sake of humans. It calls into question our responsibility for maintaining environments for future generations and asks us to consider whether it is always possible to preserve balance in nature. It also raises the question of how we might respond to habitats that have been damaged by human development.

Methodology

Before discussing the story with the children carry out some scene setting. Clarify their understanding of a rainforest and the way in which it is a sensitive ecosystem that is home to a wide range of animals. Explain that some of the plants in the illustrations can not be seen in this country, or at least, only as hothouse or house plants. Unless they have visited a hothouse at the zoo or a botanical garden it will not be easy for them to imagine what a rainforest would be like. To help them, use words like 'hot', 'damp', 'steamy', 'humid', 'wet' and 'dripping'.

Questions to ask

◆ Focus on the illustrations. Ask: How many different sorts of animals and insects can you see? The treemouse is finding it very difficult to go to sleep. Do you think the rainforest is a noisy place? Why do you think the treemouse wants to go to sleep in the day?

◆ Draw the children's attention to the pictures of the treemouse when the forest goes silent. Ask: Can you think of some words to describe how the treemouse is feeling? What is happening in the forest? Why is the treemouse so frightened by the silence?

◆ Encourage the children to focus on the illustration of the bulldozer and ask: Why do you think the bulldozer is in the middle of the forest? What is the man in the bulldozer trying to do? What will happen to the treemouse if the bulldozer carries on? What do you think made the driver stop?

◆ It says that the man sat and thought. What do you think was going through his mind? Why did he go away? Do you think he was right to go away? Why do you think he was cutting down the forest?

◆ Encourage the children to think more widely about this question. Ask: Is it right to cut down forests and destroy animal habitats? Is there any way that this could be avoided?

◆ The man left the bulldozer in the middle of the forest. What do you think will happen to it? Do you think that the treemouse and all the other animals are safe now?

◆ If you feel it to be appropriate, this story can also be used as a springboard for exploring wider global issues. It enables us to consider why trees are so important and address general issues around deforestation and global warming.

The photocopiable activity sheets

Who lives here? For this activity the children are asked to think about the ways in which other species are affected by development. It does not require a written response.

Before and after This activity is more demanding as it requires the children to think more abstractly. It does not involve any writing.

Who will lose their homes? To complete this activity the children will need to be able to write independently. The learning intention is the same as for the other activity sheets.

◆ Who lives here? ◆

- ◆ This land is going to be used to build a theme park. When this happens lots of animals and birds will lose their homes.

- ◆ Think about the creatures you think might live here and draw them in the picture.

- ◆ Draw a picture of your favourite animal in its home.

Hopscotch ◆ Caring for the environment KS1/P1–3   PHOTOCOPIABLE PAGE   33

◆ Before and after ◆

◆ Look at this picture of a theme park.

◆ Draw what you think this place might have looked like before the theme park was built.
◆ Draw pictures of the animals and birds that you think would have lived there.

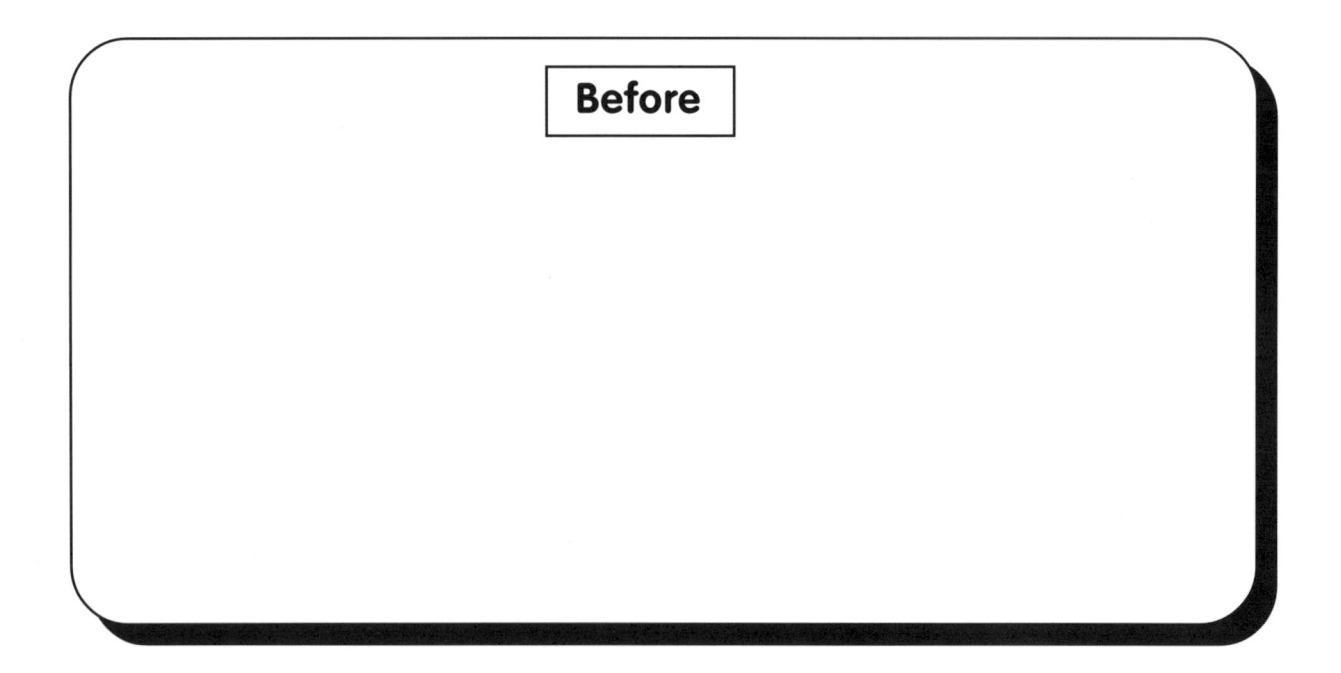

Before

PHOTOCOPIABLE PAGE   Hopscotch ◆ Caring for the environment KS1/P1–3

Who will lose their homes?

◆ When building work is done animals lose their habitats. Look at what is happening in the pictures and write some sentences to say what you think the people could do to help the animals.

Hopscotch ◆ Caring for the environment KS1/P1–3   PHOTOCOPIABLE   PAGE   35

Preserving the environment for future generations

FOCUS BOOK

WHERE THE FOREST MEETS THE SEA
by Jeannie Baker
Walker Books

INTENDED LEARNING

◆ To enhance the children's understanding of the way in which places of incredible natural beauty are in imminent danger of destruction, and how this can have enormous implications for the future.
◆ To reflect upon their personal responsibility towards the environment.

Synopsis of the story

This picture book is focused on the thoughts and feelings of a young boy as he explores a prehistoric rainforest in North Queensland, Australia. He speculates on what it would have been like millions of years ago and wonders what will happen to it in the future. The wonderful relief collages that illustrate this book depict a real place and a real predicament. The forest is part of the wilderness that meets the ocean waters of the Great Barrier Reef and it is impossible to read this book without reflecting upon what might be done to stop the destruction of the world's tropical rainforests.

Notes for teachers

This remarkable book addresses a range of issues and poses many questions. As we share it with the children we have to look at whether certain developments can be justified, and at the importance of preserving areas of natural beauty. 'Where the Forest Meets the Sea' helps children to become more aware of the ways in which development has consequences that demand our careful consideration. It sets a context in which we are asked to seriously consider our responsibilities in terms of managing a sustainable environment for future generations. In a very powerful way it helps us to realise how something that has taken millions of years to develop can be destroyed very quickly. It presents the environment as a basis for life and a source of wonder and inspiration.

Methodology

To get the most from this book it may be necessary to carry out some background work. The children will need to know what a rainforest is. They would also benefit from some insights into the Aboriginal culture. This could be done prior to or after reading the book.

Questions to ask

- Why do you think the boy and his father have to go to the rainforest by boat? (They may not understand that there are no roads into the rainforest.)
- Do you think that the rainforest is the same now as it was one hundred million years ago?
- When the boy follows the creek into the rainforest he pretends that it is a hundred million years ago. What do you think he is thinking about as he walks into the rainforest?
- Clarify the children's understanding of 'vines and creepers'. Ask: Can you think of some words that might describe this forest?
- The small boy sits still to watch and listen. What do you think he saw? What do you think he heard?
- Show the children the illustration of the hollow tree. Ask: What do you think the word 'ancient' means? What can you see in the tree?
- What do you think it might have been like to have lived in a rainforest?
- When the boy goes back to his father why does he have to follow the sound of the sea?
- Focus on the last two illustrations in the book. Ask:
    Why does the boy feel sad?
    What do you notice in the first picture?
    What do you notice in the second picture?
    What does the boy think might happen?
- Reinforce that this story is about a real place and that rainforests are being destroyed all the time. Ask:
    Why is the rainforest important?
    If it is destroyed by development can it be put back?
- Can anything can be done to halt the destruction of the rainforests?

The photocopiable activity sheets

Change This activity is intended to help the children think about the process of development. It requires no writing.

The cost of development In this activity the children are asked to focus on the consequences of development. It requires no written recording.

What would you say? This sheet requires much thought and the ability to write independently. It asks the children to consider the implications of development.

◆ Change ◆

◆ Look carefully at the pictures and then cut them out and put them in order to show how things have changed.

The cost of development

◆ Look carefully at this picture.

◆ Some of the pictures below show things that have lost their homes because of the development above.
◆ Cut out the pictures of those that have lost their homes. On another piece of paper draw a picture to show the sort of place they need to live and stick them on to your picture.

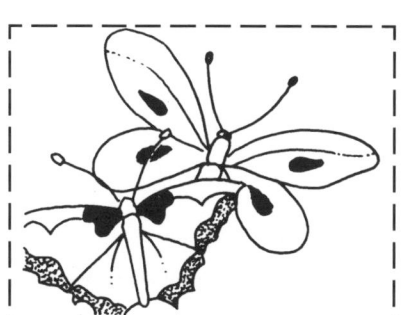

Hopscotch ◆ Caring for the environment KS1/P1–3   PHOTOCOPIABLE PAGE

◆ What would you say? ◆

- ◆ This is Victoria Jones from Jones Development Ltd. Her company wants to cut down this forest to build a shopping complex.

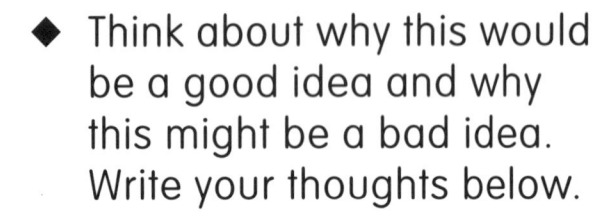

This would make an excellent site for an out of town shopping centre.

- ◆ Think about why this would be a good idea and why this might be a bad idea. Write your thoughts below.

Reasons for	Reasons against

- ◆ Compare your thoughts with those of your friend.

PHOTOCOPIABLE PAGE

Responsibility for other species

FOCUS BOOK

THE HUNTER
by Paul Geraghty
Red Fox

INTENDED LEARNING

◆ To help the children to begin to understand that hunting has far-reaching consequences that need to be given careful consideration.
◆ To appreciate the impact of hunting upon a species, for example talking about why there are now far fewer elephants than there used to be.

Synopsis of the story

Jamina wants to be a hunter. When her grandfather takes her to collect honey she pretends that she is stalking lions. As she pretends to shoot elephants and track rhinos she wanders deep into the bush. Far away she hears a desperate cry. She follows the cry and finds a baby elephant trying to wake up its dead mother. Jamina stays with the elephant and they follow the zebras across the plain until they find the baby elephant's herd.

In the morning Jamina's mother finds her sleeping in the grass. As she walks home with her mother she knows that she never wants to be a hunter.

Notes for teachers

This is an evocative and moving story about hunting and when we share this book with the children it raises many questions. Through the powerful vehicle of story the children are able to explore the consequences of animals being hunted by humans. As they empathise with the little orphaned elephant they are able to consider people's responsibilities to other species and consider whether hunting can be justified.

This is a sensitive area which needs to be handled with care and it is important to help the children understand that hunting is an issue about which not everyone will agree. It may involve us in exploring the different motivations behind hunting, for example for food, recreation, gain and control.

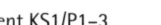

Methodology

It may be useful to set the scene for this story through a general discussion of its title – 'The Hunter'. This will enable you to find out what the children already know and think about hunting and will help you in carrying out any subsequent enquiry into the issue. Although the story focuses on elephants as a species it provides an opportunity to explore hunting more generally. Through identifying with the characters in the story the children are able to formulate ideas about what it might be like to be hunted.

Either before or after sharing the story with the children it is important to find out what they know about why people hunt elephants. This may lead to an exploration of what ivory can be used for and why the ivory trade has evolved.

Questions to ask

- Jamina said she wanted to be a hunter. Do you think she really understood what this meant?
- The hunters had killed the baby elephant's mother. Why had they not killed the baby?
- Why would the baby not be able to survive alone?
- When the baby followed Jamina it was very weak. Why was this?
- When they were by the water Jamina sensed danger. What was she afraid of and why was it not safe to cross the water?
- Show the children the illustration of the poachers. Ask: What does this picture tell us about the poachers?
- What do you think the poachers are doing?
- Jamina felt that she was one of the hunted. Why did she feel like this?
- Why did she want the baby elephant to keep quiet?
- Jamina waited to be hunted. What did she think might happen?
- Show the children the picture of Jamina as she closes her eyes and sees elephants in her dream. Draw their attention to the very edge of the picture and ask: What do you think is happening while Jamina has her eyes closed?
- How do you think Jamina felt when all the elephants arrived?
- When her mother found her the next day, Jamina said she would never be a hunter. Why do you think she said that?

The photocopiable activity sheets

Hunting happens for different reasons This activity requires no written recording. It asks the children to think about the various reasons for hunting and will need supporting by discussion.

Elephant hunters To complete this activity unsupported the children will need to be independent readers. Here again the children are asked to focus on the implications of hunting.

What would you say? For this activity the children need to be able to write independently. It also requires them to express an opinion.

Hunting happens for different reasons

- Look at the pictures. Cut out the captions below and stick them above the right picture.

| Some animals hunt for food. | Poachers hunt to make money. | Some people hunt for sport. |

Hopscotch ◆ Caring for the environment KS1/P1–3   PHOTOCOPIABLE PAGE   43

◆ Elephant hunters ◆

◆ Read the following statements. Put a tick if you think they are true. Put a cross if you think they are false.

It is alright to kill elephants. ☐

It will be hard for the baby elephant to survive if its mother is killed by the hunters. ☐

Hunters kill elephants for their ivory tusks. ☐

Hunters kill elephants for food. ☐

The hunters want to kill the baby elephant. ☐

Ivory is worth a lot of money. ☐

Hunters kill elephants for their skins. ☐

If poachers keep killing elephants there will be no elephants left. ☐

Ivory is not worth much money. ☐

The baby elephant can survive without its mother. ☐

◆ What would you say? ◆

◆ If you were watching this happen what would you want to say to the hunters. Write your answer in the speech bubble.

◆ Write some sentences to explain how you feel about hunting elephants or other wild animals.

_____
_____
_____
_____
_____
_____

Acting responsibly

♦ Make a list of the ways in which this environment might be damaged if this fire got out of control.

My list

♦ Did you remember the animals?

PHOTOCOPIABLE PAGE

Hopscotch ♦ Caring for the environment KS1/P1–3

◆ Damage to the environment ◆

◆ Put a cross by the things in this picture that are polluting the environment.

◆ Write some sentences to say what you think needs to be done to prevent some of the pollution.

_____

_____

_____

_____

_____

_____

Hopscotch ◆ Caring for the environment KS1/P1–3   PHOTOCOPIABLE PAGE